50 Hearty Oatmeal Creations

By: Kelly Johnson

Table of Contents

- Classic Maple & Brown Sugar Oatmeal
- Apple Cinnamon Oatmeal
- Peanut Butter & Banana Oatmeal
- Mixed Berry Oatmeal with Almonds
- Pumpkin Spice Oatmeal
- Chocolate Chip & Walnut Oatmeal
- Carrot Cake Oatmeal with Cream Cheese Drizzle
- Honey & Fig Oatmeal
- Blueberry Lemon Zest Oatmeal
- Chai-Spiced Oatmeal with Pecans
- Almond Joy Oatmeal with Coconut & Dark Chocolate
- Cranberry Orange Oatmeal
- Peanut Butter & Jelly Oatmeal
- Maple Pecan Oatmeal
- Mocha Oatmeal with Espresso & Cocoa
- Banana Bread Oatmeal
- Matcha Green Tea Oatmeal with Pistachios
- Strawberry Shortcake Oatmeal
- Salted Caramel & Pecan Oatmeal
- Raspberry Almond Oatmeal
- Chocolate Peanut Butter Oatmeal
- Spiced Pear & Walnut Oatmeal
- Coconut Mango Oatmeal
- Apple Pie Oatmeal with Granola Topping
- S'mores Oatmeal with Marshmallows & Graham Cracker Crumbs
- Protein-Packed Oatmeal with Greek Yogurt
- Tropical Pineapple & Coconut Oatmeal
- Maple Bacon Oatmeal
- Blackberry & Honey Oatmeal
- Cardamom & Pistachio Oatmeal
- Gingerbread Oatmeal with Molasses
- Dark Chocolate & Raspberry Oatmeal
- Cinnamon Roll Oatmeal with Vanilla Glaze
- Cashew Butter & Dates Oatmeal
- Sweet Potato Pie Oatmeal

- Cherry Almond Oatmeal
- Pine Nut & Honey Oatmeal
- Avocado & Cocoa Oatmeal
- Zucchini Bread Oatmeal with Walnuts
- Hazelnut & Dark Chocolate Oatmeal
- Tahini & Pomegranate Oatmeal
- Baked Oatmeal with Apples & Cinnamon
- Savory Oatmeal with Cheddar & Fried Egg
- Spicy Mexican Hot Chocolate Oatmeal
- Almond Butter & Dark Chocolate Oatmeal
- Turmeric Golden Milk Oatmeal
- Roasted Strawberry & Balsamic Oatmeal
- Chia & Flaxseed Superfood Oatmeal
- Lemon Poppy Seed Oatmeal
- Maple Roasted Pumpkin & Sunflower Seed Oatmeal

Classic Maple & Brown Sugar Oatmeal

Ingredients:

- 1 cup rolled oats
- 2 cups milk or water
- 2 tbsp maple syrup
- 1 tbsp brown sugar
- 1/2 tsp cinnamon (optional)

Instructions:

1. Cook oats in milk or water over medium heat until thickened.
2. Stir in maple syrup and brown sugar.
3. Serve warm with a sprinkle of cinnamon.

Apple Cinnamon Oatmeal

Ingredients:

- 1 cup rolled oats
- 2 cups milk or water
- 1/2 cup diced apples
- 1/2 tsp cinnamon
- 1 tbsp honey or maple syrup

Instructions:

1. Cook oats in milk or water.
2. Stir in apples, cinnamon, and honey.
3. Simmer for 2 minutes before serving.

Peanut Butter & Banana Oatmeal

Ingredients:

- 1 cup rolled oats
- 2 cups milk or water
- 1 tbsp peanut butter
- 1 banana, sliced
- 1 tsp honey

Instructions:

1. Cook oats in milk or water.
2. Stir in peanut butter and top with banana slices.
3. Drizzle with honey before serving.

Mixed Berry Oatmeal with Almonds

Ingredients:

- 1 cup rolled oats
- 2 cups milk or water
- 1/2 cup mixed berries (strawberries, blueberries, raspberries)
- 2 tbsp sliced almonds
- 1 tbsp honey

Instructions:

1. Cook oats in milk or water.
2. Stir in mixed berries and almonds.
3. Drizzle with honey before serving.

Pumpkin Spice Oatmeal

Ingredients:

- 1 cup rolled oats
- 2 cups milk or water
- 1/4 cup pumpkin purée
- 1/2 tsp pumpkin spice
- 1 tbsp maple syrup

Instructions:

1. Cook oats in milk or water.
2. Stir in pumpkin purée, pumpkin spice, and maple syrup.

Chocolate Chip & Walnut Oatmeal

Ingredients:

- 1 cup rolled oats
- 2 cups milk or water
- 2 tbsp chocolate chips
- 2 tbsp chopped walnuts
- 1 tsp vanilla extract

Instructions:

1. Cook oats in milk or water.
2. Stir in chocolate chips and walnuts.
3. Add vanilla before serving.

Carrot Cake Oatmeal with Cream Cheese Drizzle

Ingredients:

- 1 cup rolled oats
- 2 cups milk or water
- 1/2 cup shredded carrots
- 1/2 tsp cinnamon
- 2 tbsp raisins

Cream Cheese Drizzle:

- 2 tbsp cream cheese
- 1 tbsp honey
- 1 tbsp milk

Instructions:

1. Cook oats with carrots, cinnamon, and raisins.
2. Mix cream cheese drizzle ingredients.
3. Drizzle over oatmeal before serving.

Honey & Fig Oatmeal

Ingredients:

- 1 cup rolled oats
- 2 cups milk or water
- 2 fresh figs, sliced
- 1 tbsp honey
- 1 tbsp chopped pecans

Instructions:

1. Cook oats in milk or water.
2. Stir in figs and honey.
3. Sprinkle with pecans before serving.

Blueberry Lemon Zest Oatmeal

Ingredients:

- 1 cup rolled oats
- 2 cups milk or water
- 1/2 cup blueberries
- 1 tsp lemon zest
- 1 tbsp honey

Instructions:

1. Cook oats in milk or water.
2. Stir in blueberries and lemon zest.
3. Drizzle with honey before serving.

Chai-Spiced Oatmeal with Pecans

Ingredients:

- 1 cup rolled oats
- 2 cups milk or water
- 1/2 tsp chai spice blend
- 2 tbsp chopped pecans
- 1 tbsp maple syrup

Instructions:

1. Cook oats in milk or water.
2. Stir in chai spice blend and pecans.
3. Drizzle with maple syrup before serving.

Almond Joy Oatmeal with Coconut & Dark Chocolate

Ingredients:

- 1 cup rolled oats
- 2 cups milk or water
- 2 tbsp shredded coconut
- 1 tbsp dark chocolate chips
- 2 tbsp sliced almonds
- 1 tsp honey or maple syrup

Instructions:

1. Cook oats in milk or water.
2. Stir in shredded coconut and almonds.
3. Top with dark chocolate chips and drizzle with honey.

Cranberry Orange Oatmeal

Ingredients:

- 1 cup rolled oats
- 2 cups milk or water
- 1/4 cup dried cranberries
- 1 tsp orange zest
- 1 tbsp honey or maple syrup

Instructions:

1. Cook oats in milk or water.
2. Stir in dried cranberries and orange zest.
3. Drizzle with honey before serving.

Peanut Butter & Jelly Oatmeal

Ingredients:

- 1 cup rolled oats
- 2 cups milk or water
- 1 tbsp peanut butter
- 1 tbsp fruit preserves (strawberry or raspberry)
- 1/2 banana, sliced (optional)

Instructions:

1. Cook oats in milk or water.
2. Swirl in peanut butter and fruit preserves.
3. Top with banana slices if desired.

Maple Pecan Oatmeal

Ingredients:

- 1 cup rolled oats
- 2 cups milk or water
- 2 tbsp chopped pecans
- 1 tbsp maple syrup
- 1/2 tsp cinnamon

Instructions:

1. Cook oats in milk or water.
2. Stir in pecans and cinnamon.
3. Drizzle with maple syrup before serving.

Mocha Oatmeal with Espresso & Cocoa

Ingredients:

- 1 cup rolled oats
- 1 1/2 cups milk or water
- 1/2 cup brewed espresso or strong coffee
- 1 tbsp cocoa powder
- 1 tbsp maple syrup or honey

Instructions:

1. Cook oats in milk and espresso.
2. Stir in cocoa powder and maple syrup.

Banana Bread Oatmeal

Ingredients:

- 1 cup rolled oats
- 2 cups milk or water
- 1 ripe banana, mashed
- 1/2 tsp cinnamon
- 1 tbsp chopped walnuts

Instructions:

1. Cook oats in milk or water.
2. Stir in mashed banana and cinnamon.
3. Top with walnuts before serving.

Matcha Green Tea Oatmeal with Pistachios

Ingredients:

- 1 cup rolled oats
- 2 cups milk or water
- 1 tsp matcha green tea powder
- 1 tbsp honey
- 2 tbsp chopped pistachios

Instructions:

1. Cook oats in milk or water.
2. Stir in matcha powder and honey.
3. Top with chopped pistachios.

Strawberry Shortcake Oatmeal

Ingredients:

- 1 cup rolled oats
- 2 cups milk or water
- 1/2 cup fresh strawberries, chopped
- 1 tbsp Greek yogurt or whipped cream
- 1 tsp vanilla extract
- 1 tbsp honey

Instructions:

1. Cook oats in milk or water.
2. Stir in vanilla extract and strawberries.
3. Top with Greek yogurt and drizzle with honey.

Salted Caramel & Pecan Oatmeal

Ingredients:

- 1 cup rolled oats
- 2 cups milk or water
- 2 tbsp chopped pecans
- 1 tbsp caramel sauce
- 1/2 tsp sea salt

Instructions:

1. Cook oats in milk or water.
2. Stir in caramel sauce and pecans.
3. Sprinkle with sea salt before serving.

Raspberry Almond Oatmeal

Ingredients:

- 1 cup rolled oats
- 2 cups milk or water
- 1/2 cup fresh or frozen raspberries
- 2 tbsp sliced almonds
- 1 tbsp honey

Instructions:

1. Cook oats in milk or water.
2. Stir in raspberries and almonds.
3. Drizzle with honey before serving.

Chocolate Peanut Butter Oatmeal

Ingredients:

- 1 cup rolled oats
- 2 cups milk or water
- 1 tbsp cocoa powder
- 1 tbsp peanut butter
- 1 tbsp honey or maple syrup
- 1 tbsp dark chocolate chips (optional)

Instructions:

1. Cook oats in milk or water.
2. Stir in cocoa powder, peanut butter, and sweetener.
3. Top with dark chocolate chips before serving.

Spiced Pear & Walnut Oatmeal

Ingredients:

- 1 cup rolled oats
- 2 cups milk or water
- 1/2 cup diced pear
- 1/2 tsp cinnamon
- 1/4 tsp nutmeg
- 2 tbsp chopped walnuts
- 1 tbsp honey

Instructions:

1. Cook oats in milk or water.
2. Stir in diced pear, cinnamon, and nutmeg.
3. Top with walnuts and drizzle with honey.

Coconut Mango Oatmeal

Ingredients:

- 1 cup rolled oats
- 2 cups coconut milk or water
- 1/2 cup fresh or frozen mango, diced
- 2 tbsp shredded coconut
- 1 tsp honey or maple syrup

Instructions:

1. Cook oats in coconut milk or water.
2. Stir in mango and shredded coconut.
3. Drizzle with honey before serving.

Apple Pie Oatmeal with Granola Topping

Ingredients:

- 1 cup rolled oats
- 2 cups milk or water
- 1/2 cup diced apples
- 1/2 tsp cinnamon
- 1 tbsp brown sugar
- 1/4 cup granola

Instructions:

1. Cook oats in milk or water.
2. Stir in apples, cinnamon, and brown sugar.
3. Top with granola for crunch.

S'mores Oatmeal with Marshmallows & Graham Cracker Crumbs

Ingredients:

- 1 cup rolled oats
- 2 cups milk or water
- 1 tbsp cocoa powder
- 2 tbsp mini marshmallows
- 1 tbsp graham cracker crumbs
- 1 tbsp chocolate chips

Instructions:

1. Cook oats in milk or water.
2. Stir in cocoa powder.
3. Top with marshmallows, graham cracker crumbs, and chocolate chips.

Protein-Packed Oatmeal with Greek Yogurt

Ingredients:

- 1 cup rolled oats
- 2 cups milk or water
- 1/2 cup Greek yogurt
- 1 tbsp honey
- 1 tbsp chia seeds

Instructions:

1. Cook oats in milk or water.
2. Stir in Greek yogurt and honey.
3. Sprinkle with chia seeds before serving.

Tropical Pineapple & Coconut Oatmeal

Ingredients:

- 1 cup rolled oats
- 2 cups coconut milk or water
- 1/2 cup diced pineapple
- 2 tbsp shredded coconut
- 1 tsp honey

Instructions:

1. Cook oats in coconut milk or water.
2. Stir in pineapple and shredded coconut.
3. Drizzle with honey before serving.

Maple Bacon Oatmeal

Ingredients:

- 1 cup rolled oats
- 2 cups milk or water
- 2 tbsp maple syrup
- 2 strips crispy bacon, crumbled
- 1/2 tsp sea salt

Instructions:

1. Cook oats in milk or water.
2. Stir in maple syrup.
3. Top with crumbled bacon and sea salt.

Blackberry & Honey Oatmeal

Ingredients:

- 1 cup rolled oats
- 2 cups milk or water
- 1/2 cup blackberries
- 1 tbsp honey
- 1/2 tsp vanilla extract

Instructions:

1. Cook oats in milk or water.
2. Stir in vanilla extract.
3. Top with blackberries and drizzle with honey.

Cardamom & Pistachio Oatmeal

Ingredients:

- 1 cup rolled oats
- 2 cups milk or water
- 1/2 tsp ground cardamom
- 2 tbsp chopped pistachios
- 1 tbsp honey or maple syrup

Instructions:

1. Cook oats in milk or water.
2. Stir in cardamom.
3. Top with pistachios and drizzle with honey.

Gingerbread Oatmeal with Molasses

Ingredients:

- 1 cup rolled oats
- 2 cups milk or water
- 1 tbsp molasses
- 1/2 tsp ground ginger
- 1/2 tsp cinnamon
- 1 tbsp brown sugar
- 1 tbsp chopped pecans (optional)

Instructions:

1. Cook oats in milk or water.
2. Stir in molasses, ginger, cinnamon, and brown sugar.
3. Top with chopped pecans if desired.

Dark Chocolate & Raspberry Oatmeal

Ingredients:

- 1 cup rolled oats
- 2 cups milk or water
- 2 tbsp dark chocolate chips
- 1/2 cup fresh or frozen raspberries
- 1 tsp honey or maple syrup

Instructions:

1. Cook oats in milk or water.
2. Stir in dark chocolate chips until melted.
3. Top with raspberries and drizzle with honey.

Cinnamon Roll Oatmeal with Vanilla Glaze

Ingredients:

- 1 cup rolled oats
- 2 cups milk or water
- 1 tsp cinnamon
- 1 tbsp brown sugar
- 1/2 tsp vanilla extract

Vanilla Glaze:

- 2 tbsp powdered sugar
- 1 tsp milk
- 1/4 tsp vanilla extract

Instructions:

1. Cook oats in milk or water with cinnamon and brown sugar.
2. Mix glaze ingredients and drizzle over oatmeal.

Cashew Butter & Dates Oatmeal

Ingredients:

- 1 cup rolled oats
- 2 cups milk or water
- 1 tbsp cashew butter
- 3 dates, chopped
- 1/2 tsp cinnamon

Instructions:

1. Cook oats in milk or water.
2. Stir in cashew butter and cinnamon.
3. Top with chopped dates before serving.

Sweet Potato Pie Oatmeal

Ingredients:

- 1 cup rolled oats
- 2 cups milk or water
- 1/2 cup mashed sweet potato
- 1/2 tsp pumpkin pie spice
- 1 tbsp maple syrup
- 1 tbsp chopped pecans

Instructions:

1. Cook oats in milk or water.
2. Stir in mashed sweet potato, pumpkin pie spice, and maple syrup.
3. Top with pecans before serving.

Cherry Almond Oatmeal

Ingredients:

- 1 cup rolled oats
- 2 cups milk or water
- 1/2 cup fresh or dried cherries
- 2 tbsp sliced almonds
- 1 tbsp honey

Instructions:

1. Cook oats in milk or water.
2. Stir in cherries and almonds.
3. Drizzle with honey before serving.

Pine Nut & Honey Oatmeal

Ingredients:

- 1 cup rolled oats
- 2 cups milk or water
- 2 tbsp pine nuts
- 1 tbsp honey
- 1/2 tsp cinnamon

Instructions:

1. Cook oats in milk or water.
2. Stir in cinnamon.
3. Top with pine nuts and drizzle with honey.

Avocado & Cocoa Oatmeal *(Creamy & Rich!)*

Ingredients:

- 1 cup rolled oats
- 2 cups milk or water
- 1/2 ripe avocado, mashed
- 1 tbsp cocoa powder
- 1 tbsp maple syrup

Instructions:

1. Cook oats in milk or water.
2. Stir in mashed avocado, cocoa powder, and maple syrup.

Zucchini Bread Oatmeal with Walnuts

Ingredients:

- 1 cup rolled oats
- 2 cups milk or water
- 1/2 cup grated zucchini
- 1/2 tsp cinnamon
- 1 tbsp brown sugar
- 2 tbsp chopped walnuts

Instructions:

1. Cook oats in milk or water.
2. Stir in zucchini, cinnamon, and brown sugar.
3. Top with walnuts before serving.

Hazelnut & Dark Chocolate Oatmeal

Ingredients:

- 1 cup rolled oats
- 2 cups milk or water
- 2 tbsp chopped hazelnuts
- 2 tbsp dark chocolate chips
- 1/2 tsp vanilla extract

Instructions:

1. Cook oats in milk or water.
2. Stir in hazelnuts and vanilla extract.
3. Top with dark chocolate chips before serving.

Tahini & Pomegranate Oatmeal

Ingredients:

- 1 cup rolled oats
- 2 cups milk or water
- 1 tbsp tahini
- 2 tbsp pomegranate seeds
- 1 tsp honey
- 1/2 tsp cinnamon

Instructions:

1. Cook oats in milk or water.
2. Stir in tahini and cinnamon.
3. Top with pomegranate seeds and drizzle with honey.

Baked Oatmeal with Apples & Cinnamon

Ingredients:

- 2 cups rolled oats
- 1 1/2 cups milk
- 1 apple, diced
- 1/2 tsp cinnamon
- 1 tbsp maple syrup
- 1/2 tsp baking powder
- 1 egg (optional, for extra structure)

Instructions:

1. Preheat oven to **375°F (190°C)**.
2. Mix all ingredients in a baking dish.
3. Bake for **25-30 minutes** until golden brown.

Savory Oatmeal with Cheddar & Fried Egg

Ingredients:

- 1 cup rolled oats
- 2 cups water or broth
- 1/4 cup shredded cheddar cheese
- 1 fried egg
- 1/2 tsp black pepper
- 1 tbsp green onions, chopped

Instructions:

1. Cook oats in water or broth.
2. Stir in cheddar cheese and black pepper.
3. Top with a fried egg and green onions.

Spicy Mexican Hot Chocolate Oatmeal

Ingredients:

- 1 cup rolled oats
- 2 cups milk
- 1 tbsp cocoa powder
- 1/2 tsp cinnamon
- 1/4 tsp cayenne pepper
- 1 tbsp honey
- 1 tbsp dark chocolate chips

Instructions:

1. Cook oats in milk.
2. Stir in cocoa, cinnamon, cayenne, and honey.
3. Top with dark chocolate chips.

Almond Butter & Dark Chocolate Oatmeal

Ingredients:

- 1 cup rolled oats
- 2 cups milk or water
- 1 tbsp almond butter
- 2 tbsp dark chocolate chunks
- 1/2 tsp vanilla extract

Instructions:

1. Cook oats in milk or water.
2. Stir in almond butter and vanilla.
3. Top with dark chocolate chunks.

Turmeric Golden Milk Oatmeal

Ingredients:

- 1 cup rolled oats
- 2 cups almond milk
- 1/2 tsp turmeric
- 1/4 tsp cinnamon
- 1/4 tsp black pepper
- 1 tbsp honey

Instructions:

1. Cook oats in almond milk.
2. Stir in turmeric, cinnamon, black pepper, and honey.

Roasted Strawberry & Balsamic Oatmeal

Ingredients:

- 1 cup rolled oats
- 2 cups milk or water
- 1/2 cup strawberries, halved
- 1 tbsp balsamic glaze
- 1 tbsp honey

Instructions:

1. Roast strawberries at **375°F (190°C) for 15 minutes**.
2. Cook oats in milk or water.
3. Top with roasted strawberries and drizzle with balsamic glaze and honey.

Chia & Flaxseed Superfood Oatmeal

Ingredients:

- 1 cup rolled oats
- 2 cups almond milk
- 1 tbsp chia seeds
- 1 tbsp flaxseeds
- 1 tbsp honey or maple syrup

Instructions:

1. Cook oats in almond milk.
2. Stir in chia seeds and flaxseeds.
3. Drizzle with honey before serving.

Lemon Poppy Seed Oatmeal

Ingredients:

- 1 cup rolled oats
- 2 cups milk or water
- 1 tsp lemon zest
- 1/2 tsp vanilla extract
- 1 tbsp poppy seeds
- 1 tbsp honey

Instructions:

1. Cook oats in milk or water.
2. Stir in lemon zest, vanilla, and poppy seeds.
3. Drizzle with honey before serving.

Maple Roasted Pumpkin & Sunflower Seed Oatmeal

Ingredients:

- 1 cup rolled oats
- 2 cups milk or water
- 1/2 cup roasted pumpkin cubes
- 2 tbsp sunflower seeds
- 1 tbsp maple syrup

Instructions:

1. Roast pumpkin cubes at **375°F (190°C) for 20 minutes** with a drizzle of maple syrup.
2. Cook oats in milk or water.
3. Top with roasted pumpkin and sunflower seeds.

www.ingramcontent.com/pod-product-compliance
Lightning Source LLC
LaVergne TN
LVHW061954070526
838199LV00060B/4122